AF477317

BUILDING WINNING STRATEGIES WITH

ANALYTICS

Adeyeha Temitope

A catalogue record for this book is available at the National Library of Nigeria.

TABLE OF CONTENT

FOREWORD

In today's rapidly evolving business landscape, the phrase "data is the new oil" is not merely a buzzword but a reality that businesses and organizations are coming to terms with. Over the past few decades, analytics has shifted from being a specialized field for statisticians and scientists into a strategic cornerstone that affects decision-making across every sector. Businesses today no longer rely on intuition or past experiences alone to guide their paths forward. Instead, they leverage the power of data and analytics to craft strategies that are informed, dynamic, and results oriented. This transformation in how decisions are made is particularly fascinating because it signifies a shift in the very DNA of companies. Data is no longer just a tool—it's a guiding force that influences everything from product development to customer service, financial planning, and beyond. Analytics has evolved into a powerful instrument, capable of giving businesses the competitive edge needed to thrive in saturated markets, navigate complex financial landscapes, and engage more meaningfully with their customers. It's no exaggeration to say that companies that fail to embrace analytics risk being left behind.

When I first began working with analytics, the landscape was vastly different. The tools were rudimentary, the data sets were smaller, and the challenges were largely around the collection and storage of data. Now, we live in a world where data is not just available but is being generated at an unprecedented scale—from the clicks on websites to the transactions at a store, from social media interactions to the emails we send every day. This abundance of data presents both opportunities and challenges. While there is more data available, not every organization knows how to use it effectively to drive strategies and outcomes. That's where this book comes in. **"Building Winning Strategies with Analytics"** does more than just provide a deep dive into the world of data; it offers a practical, easy-to-follow guide for how to use data to shape decisions that propel organizations toward success. Whether you are a seasoned data professional or a business leader looking to integrate analytics into your operations, this book provides valuable insights that can transform your strategic planning processes. One of the key strengths of this book is its multi-disciplinary approach.

It doesn't limit itself to just one area, such as finance or marketing. Instead, it spans across business strategy, financial planning, marketing optimization, and even project launches. The author recognizes that analytics is not confined to a single domain; it's a powerful tool that has applications in virtually every sector of business and society. By providing a comprehensive view, the book becomes a valuable resource for anyone who wants to understand how analytics can be used to make smarter, more effective decisions in a variety of contexts. The integration of analytics into strategic decision-making has long been recognized as a game changer, but as this book will reveal, it is not just about the numbers. It's about creating a culture within an organization that values data-driven insights. For businesses to fully leverage analytics, there must be a fundamental shift in mindset—one that prioritizes fact-based decision-making over intuition or hierarchy. This cultural shift is arguably the most important factor in driving successful analytics strategies. Without it, even the best tools and the most advanced algorithms will fall short.

As you read through the chapters of this book, you'll find real-world examples and case studies that illustrate the practical applications of analytics. The book is filled with actionable insights and proven techniques that you can apply immediately to your own business context. Whether you are trying to forecast financial trends, optimize a marketing campaign, or scale a new project launch, the lessons contained here will provide a strong foundation. One of the most significant aspects of this book is its accessibility. The concepts of analytics and data science can sometimes feel intimidating, especially for those who don't come from a technical background. However, the author has done an exceptional job of breaking down complex ideas into simple, digestible parts. This makes it not only easy to follow but also engaging for readers at every level of expertise. Whether you are a beginner in the field of data analytics or an experienced professional, you'll find this book both informative and inspiring. I encourage you to approach this book with an open mind and a willingness to challenge some of the traditional ways of thinking about strategy.

The future belongs to organizations that can adapt quickly, pivot when necessary, and make decisions based on solid, data-driven insights. Analytics offers that competitive advantage, and the strategies outlined in this book will show you how to harness its full potential. I believe the knowledge shared in these pages will equip you with the tools and mindset necessary to navigate the complexities of today's business environment, making smarter, faster, and more informed decisions. You'll come away with not just theoretical understanding but practical skills that can be implemented right away. So, whether you're leading a Fortune 500 company or launching your first startup, the principles in **"Building Winning Strategies with Analytics"** will help you create strategies that are not just winning but sustainable. It is an indispensable guide for anyone serious about succeeding in today's data-driven world.

"Without data, you're just another person with an opinion."
– W. Edwards Deming

"In God we trust, all others must bring data."
– W. Edwards Deming

"The goal is to turn data into information, and information into insight."
– Carly Fiorina

"Numbers have an important story to tell. They rely on you to give them a clear and convincing voice."
– Stephen Few

INTRODUCTION

In the age of information, data has become a crucial asset for individuals and organizations alike. Companies across the world are realizing that the key to gaining a competitive edge lies in their ability to harness and analyze vast amounts of data. Whether it's understanding customer behavior, predicting market trends, or optimizing internal processes, analytics offers the insights necessary to make informed decisions and craft winning strategies. But what does it mean to build a winning strategy with analytics? For many, the concept of data-driven decision-making remains abstract. It's easy to see the value of data but applying it in a way that leads to tangible, actionable results can feel daunting. This book aims to bridge that gap. It is designed to demystify the world of analytics and show you, step by step, how to leverage data to create strategies that work—whether in business, finance, marketing, or launching new projects. One of the most powerful aspects of analytics is its versatility. While each industry has its unique challenges, the fundamental principles of data-driven strategy apply across sectors.

Whether you're trying to forecast financial performance, optimize your marketing campaigns, or ensure the success of a new product launch, analytics provides the tools to back your decisions with evidence and precision. Over the next ten chapters, we will explore how businesses across various industries use analytics to their advantage. We will dive into real-world examples that illustrate how organizations have successfully integrated data into their strategic planning processes and examine the challenges they faced along the way. At its core, this book is not just for data scientists or technical professionals. It's for anyone looking to use data to make better decisions, improve business outcomes, and navigate the complexities of today's fast-paced, data-driven world. Whether you are a business leader, a financial planner, a marketing professional, or someone launching a new project, the principles of analytics can help you unlock new opportunities, solve problems, and create sustainable growth. This is not a book about the technicalities of data science. Instead, it focuses on the practical applications of analytics—the "how" and "why" of using data to build strategies that win.

The goal is to make the subject accessible and actionable, providing you with insights that can be applied immediately, no matter what your level of expertise with data. As you begin this journey, remember that data is not just about numbers; it's about understanding the stories those numbers tell. By the end of this book, you will have the knowledge and confidence to transform data into a strategic asset, helping you to make decisions that are informed, effective, and sustainable.

Welcome to Building Winning Strategies with Analytics—your guide to thriving in the age of data.

CHAPTER 1

The Role of Analytics in Business Strategy

In today's business environment, data and analytics have become indispensable tools for companies looking to stay competitive and drive growth. The ability to collect, analyze, and interpret data allows organizations to make more informed decisions, adapt to changes in the market, and optimize their operations. Yet, despite the widespread availability of data, many businesses struggle to integrate analytics into their strategic planning processes effectively. Analytics plays a pivotal role in shaping business strategy because it transforms raw data into actionable insights. These insights help businesses understand their customers, identify emerging trends, streamline operations, and even forecast future challenges. However, to fully harness the power of analytics, organizations need to cultivate a data-driven culture and develop a strategic approach that aligns analytics with their overall business objectives. At its core, the role of analytics in business strategy can be broken down into several key areas: decision-making, performance optimization, competitive advantage, and innovation.

Data-Driven Decision-Making

One of the most significant contributions of analytics to business strategy is the shift from intuition-based decisions to data-driven decision-making. In the past, many business leaders relied on their experience, gut feelings, or anecdotal evidence to make strategic choices. While these approaches may have worked in simpler, less complex times, the modern business landscape demands a more rigorous approach. Data-driven decision-making enables leaders to base their choices on evidence, reducing the risk of costly mistakes and increasing the likelihood of success. For example, when launching a new product, businesses can use analytics to conduct market research, identify customer preferences, and assess the competitive landscape. Rather than making assumptions about what customers want, data allows companies to validate their ideas and tailor their products or services to meet actual demand. This reduces uncertainty and helps businesses launch products that are more likely to succeed. Moreover, analytics can help businesses evaluate the effectiveness of their existing strategies. By analyzing key performance indicators (KPIs) and other metrics, companies can determine whether their current approaches are delivering the desired outcomes. If not, they can adjust their strategies based on data-driven insights, rather than relying on trial and error.

Optimizing Performance

In addition to improving decision-making, analytics is instrumental in optimizing business performance. Whether it's enhancing operational efficiency, improving customer satisfaction, or increasing profitability, data can provide valuable insights into areas where a business can improve. For instance, analytics can be used to streamline supply chain operations by identifying bottlenecks or inefficiencies in the production process. By analyzing data from various stages of the supply chain, companies can pinpoint where delays or resource waste are occurring, allowing them to make targeted improvements. Similarly, in customer service, analytics can reveal common pain points or areas where customers experience dissatisfaction. By addressing these issues, businesses can enhance the overall customer experience and increase loyalty. Performance optimization also extends to financial management. Analytics can help businesses identify cost-saving opportunities, optimize pricing strategies, and improve cash flow management. By analyzing financial data, companies can uncover patterns and trends that may not be immediately apparent, leading to better financial decision-making.

Gaining a Competitive Advantage

In a crowded marketplace, gaining a competitive edge is crucial for long-term success. Analytics offers businesses the tools to stay ahead of the competition by providing insights into market trends, customer behavior, and industry shifts. One of the ways analytics contributes to competitive advantage is through predictive modeling. By analyzing historical data, businesses can develop models that forecast future trends, allowing them to anticipate changes in customer demand, market conditions, or industry regulations. This foresight enables companies to be proactive rather than reactive, giving them a distinct advantage over competitors who may be slower to adapt. Additionally, analytics can be used to monitor competitor performance. By tracking publicly available data, such as financial reports, marketing campaigns, or customer reviews, businesses can gain valuable insights into their competitors' strengths and weaknesses. This information can inform strategic decisions, such as entering new markets or adjusting pricing strategies, to capitalize on opportunities that competitors may have overlooked. Another critical aspect of gaining a competitive advantage is personalization. With the rise of digital technology, customers increasingly expect personalized experiences tailored to their individual needs and preferences. Analytics allows businesses to segment their customer base and deliver targeted marketing campaigns, product recommendations, or customer service interactions. Personalization not only enhances the customer experience but also increases conversion rates and drives customer loyalty.

Promoting Innovation

Innovation is at the heart of business success, and analytics plays a key role in fostering a culture of innovation within organizations. By analyzing data from various sources, companies can identify new opportunities for growth, whether it's developing new products, entering new markets, or improving existing services. Data-driven innovation often starts with customer feedback. By analyzing customer interactions, reviews, and social media conversations, businesses can gain insights into unmet needs or emerging trends. These insights can then be used to inform product development or service enhancements. For example, a company might discover that customers are seeking a faster, more convenient way to access their services, leading to the development of a new app or feature that addresses this demand. Additionally, analytics can be used to explore new market opportunities. By analyzing demographic, geographic, or behavioral data, companies can identify potential customer segments that they may not have previously considered. This data-driven approach to market expansion reduces the risk of entering new markets and increases the likelihood of success. Furthermore, analytics can help businesses measure the impact of their innovations. By tracking key metrics, such as customer adoption rates or revenue growth, companies can assess the effectiveness of their new products or services and make adjustments as needed. This iterative approach to innovation ensures that businesses are constantly improving and staying ahead of the competition.

Building a Data-Driven Culture

For businesses to fully realize the benefits of analytics, it's essential to foster a data-driven culture. This involves more than just investing in the latest tools or technologies; it requires a mindset shift across the entire organization. Employees at all levels need to understand the value of data and how to use it to inform their decisions. One of the challenges in building a data-driven culture is overcoming resistance to change. Some employees may be hesitant to rely on data, preferring to stick with familiar methods of decision-making. To address this, organizations need to provide training and support to help employees develop their data literacy skills. Additionally, leaders must lead by example, demonstrating how data can be used to drive better outcomes. Creating a data-driven culture also involves breaking down silos within the organization. Data needs to flow freely across departments to ensure that everyone has access to the information they need. This requires a collaborative approach to data management, where teams work together to share insights and develop cross-functional strategies.

CHAPTER 2

Understanding Data

Data is the foundation upon which all analytics is built, making it one of the most critical components of any business strategy. Before diving into the practical applications of analytics, it's essential to develop a thorough understanding of what data is, how it is collected, and the different types of data businesses rely on. Data, in its simplest form, is information—whether numerical, textual, or graphically collected from various sources. When properly analyzed, data provides insights that drive decisions, shape strategies, and predict future trends. However, not all data is created equal, and the quality, type, and source of data can significantly impact the outcomes of an analysis. In this chapter, we'll explore the different types of data, the importance of data quality, data collection techniques, and data management processes. By the end, you'll have a clearer understanding of how to use data effectively within your organization.

The Different Types of Data

One of the first steps in understanding data is recognizing that it comes in many forms. The most common way to categorize data is by its structure, which can be broken down into three primary types: structured data, unstructured data, and semi-structured data.

Structured Data: Structured data refers to data that is highly organized and easily searchable in databases or spreadsheets. This type of data fits neatly into rows and columns, making it straightforward to analyze. Examples of structured data include financial records, inventory lists, and customer contact information. Because structured data is organized, it is relatively easy to process and analyze using traditional statistical methods or more advanced analytics tools. Businesses often rely on structured data for day-to-day operations and strategic decision-making. For example, a company might use sales data to determine which products are performing well or analyze employee productivity data to identify areas for improvement. Since structured data is the most accessible and widely used form, it is typically the starting point for many organizations' analytics efforts.

Unstructured Data: Unstructured data, on the other hand, does not fit neatly into rows and columns. This type of data includes information that is more difficult to organize, such as emails, social media posts, video files, and customer reviews. Despite its lack of structure, unstructured data is incredibly valuable because it often contains rich insights that cannot be captured by traditional data points. With the rise of digital communication and social media, businesses are increasingly dealing with large volumes of unstructured data. While this data may be challenging to analyze, it offers a wealth of information about customer preferences, sentiment, and behavior. For instance, analyzing customer reviews on social media platforms can provide companies with insights into how their products or services are perceived by the public. Because of the complexity of unstructured data, businesses often use advanced analytics techniques, such as natural language processing (NLP) or machine learning algorithms, to extract meaningful insights. These tools help convert unstructured data into actionable information, allowing businesses to make more informed decisions.

Semi-Structured Data: Semi-structured data is a hybrid of structured and unstructured data. While it doesn't fit perfectly into traditional database structures, it still contains organizational elements, such as tags or metadata, that make it easier to manage and analyze than purely unstructured data. Examples of semi-structured data include XML files, emails with tags, or JSON data from web applications. Semi-structured data plays a critical role in many business processes, particularly in industries that rely heavily on digital communication or complex data systems. For example, an eCommerce company might use semi-structured data to track customer transactions, product inventory, and shipping information, all of which may not be stored in traditional relational databases.

The Importance of Data Quality

While understanding the types of data is essential, ensuring that the data you collect is of high quality is equally critical. Poor-quality data can lead to inaccurate analyses, flawed insights, and misguided decision-making. Therefore, businesses must invest in practices that ensure the data they are using is accurate, complete, and reliable.

Several key dimensions define data quality:

Accuracy: Data must be an accurate representation of the real-world events or objects it describes. For example, incorrect customer contact information or inaccurate sales figures can lead to faulty analysis.

Completeness: Incomplete data sets can skew analysis results. Missing values or incomplete data entries limit the scope of what can be learned from the data.

Consistency: Data consistency refers to how well data aligns across different sources and timeframes. Inconsistent data, such as varying product codes or conflicting customer records, can make it difficult to draw meaningful insights.

Timeliness: For data to be useful, it must be up to date. Outdated information can lead to decisions based on irrelevant or obsolete trends.

Validity: Data must adhere to defined formats and standards. Invalid data, such as text entered into a numeric field, can lead to errors during analysis.

To ensure data quality, businesses must implement robust data governance practices. This includes establishing clear data entry protocols, conducting regular audits of data systems, and investing in data cleaning tools that can automatically detect and correct errors. Without high-quality data, even the most sophisticated analytics tools will produce unreliable results.

Data Collection Techniques

The process of gathering data is one of the most crucial aspects of building a data-driven strategy. Data collection involves capturing information from various sources and ensuring that the data is relevant to the business' needs. There are multiple techniques for collecting data, ranging from traditional methods like surveys and interviews to modern techniques such as web scraping, sensor data collection, and automated data logging.

Primary Data Collection: Primary data is information collected directly from the source for a specific purpose. This data is often gathered through methods like surveys, interviews, focus groups, or direct observations. The advantage of primary data is that it is highly relevant to the business's needs because it is tailored to answer specific questions or solve particular problems. For example, a company launching a new product might conduct a survey to gather customer opinions and preferences. This primary data helps the company understand its target audience and refine its product offerings accordingly. However, primary data collection can be time-consuming and expensive, which is why businesses often complement it with secondary data collection.

Secondary Data Collection: This refers to information that has already been collected by another source, such as government agencies, market research firms, or academic institutions. This type of data is often less expensive and faster to obtain than primary data, but it may not be as directly relevant to a company's specific needs. Businesses commonly use secondary data to supplement their primary data collection efforts. For example, a company might use market research reports to gain insights into industry trends or rely on publicly available financial data to benchmark its performance against competitors. Both primary and secondary data collection have their advantages and disadvantages. To maximize the effectiveness of their data strategy, businesses must carefully consider which method (or combination of methods) is best suited to their specific goals.

Managing Data Effectively

Once data is collected, it must be properly stored, managed, and analyzed. Data management involves organizing data in a way that makes it easily accessible, ensuring its security, and maintaining its quality over time. With the rise of big data, effective data management has become increasingly important, as businesses deal with larger and more complex data sets than ever before. One of the most critical aspects of data management is choosing the right storage system. There are several options available, including traditional databases, data warehouses, and cloud storage solutions. The choice of storage depends on the type and volume of data a business collects, as well as its specific needs for access, security, and scalability. In addition to storage, businesses must invest in data security to protect sensitive information from unauthorized access or breaches. This includes implementing encryption, access controls, and regular security audits to ensure that data is protected at all times. Finally, businesses must prioritize data maintenance to ensure that the information they rely on remains accurate and up to date. This involves regularly updating records, removing duplicates, and addressing inconsistencies.

CHAPTER 3

Analytics for Financial Success

Financial success in today's complex business landscape depends heavily on the ability to make informed, data-driven decisions. Analytics provides a powerful set of tools to improve financial planning, enhance forecasting accuracy, identify risks, and optimize investment strategies. As the financial environment grows increasingly competitive and interconnected, businesses that leverage data analytics gain a distinct advantage over those that continue to rely solely on traditional financial management techniques. This chapter explores how organizations can use analytics to gain insights into their financial health, make more informed decisions, mitigate risks, and ultimately drive long-term financial success. We'll cover various aspects of financial analytics, from budgeting and forecasting to risk management and portfolio optimization. By the end of this chapter, you'll understand how to harness the power of data to transform financial decision-making into your organization.

The Role of Analytics in Financial Planning

Financial planning is a critical function for any organization, whether it's a startup looking to raise capital or a multinational corporation managing multiple revenue streams. Traditionally, financial planning was driven by historical data and expert intuition. While these methods provide valuable context, they often fall short in today's rapidly changing market. Analytics offers a more dynamic approach to financial planning, allowing organizations to create more accurate and adaptable financial models. One of the most significant benefits of using analytics in financial planning is the ability to develop data-driven budgets. Rather than basing a budget solely on last year's numbers or assumptions, analytics enables businesses to account for a wide range of variables, such as market trends, consumer behavior, and operational costs. By analyzing these factors, companies can develop more realistic budgets that better reflect future financial needs.

For instance, predictive analytics can be used to forecast revenue and expenses based on historical data combined with real-time market conditions. This allows businesses to anticipate changes in demand, price fluctuations, and other factors that impact financial performance. The result is a more agile and responsive financial plan that can be adjusted as new data becomes available. Moreover, financial analytics helps organizations optimize resource allocation. By analyzing spending patterns, cash flow, and profitability, businesses can identify areas where resources are being underutilized or where investments are generating suboptimal returns. This insight enables companies to reallocate resources toward more profitable ventures, ensuring that every dollar spent contributes to overall financial success.

Forecasting with Financial Analytics

Forecasting is a cornerstone of financial success. Accurate forecasting allows businesses to anticipate future financial performance, adjust strategies in response to market shifts, and make more informed decisions about investments and growth. However, traditional forecasting methods are often limited by their reliance on historical data and static models. In contrast, financial analytics enables organizations to create dynamic forecasts that account for a broader range of factors and provide more accurate predictions. One of the most valuable tools in financial forecasting is predictive analytics. By analyzing historical data and using statistical models, predictive analytics can forecast future outcomes with a higher degree of accuracy than traditional methods. For example, predictive analytics can be used to forecast sales revenue, customer demand, or cash flow based on patterns in past performance combined with external variables, such as economic indicators or industry trends.

Another key advantage of using analytics in forecasting is the ability to perform scenario analysis. Scenario analysis allows businesses to model different financial outcomes based on various assumptions or potential events. For example, a company might create multiple financial scenarios based on different economic conditions, such as a recession, a boom in consumer spending, or fluctuations in currency exchange rates. By analyzing these scenarios, businesses can identify potential risks and opportunities, enabling them to prepare for a range of outcomes. In addition to predictive analytics, businesses can also use descriptive analytics to gain insights into past performance and identify trends. Descriptive analytics involves analyzing historical data to understand what has happened in the past and why it occurred. This type of analysis is particularly useful for identifying patterns or anomalies in financial data, such as seasonal fluctuations in sales or unexpected changes in costs. By understanding these trends, businesses can develop more accurate forecasts and make better strategic decisions.

Managing Financial Risks with Analytics

Risk management is another critical area where analytics plays a vital role. Every business faces financial risks, whether it's market volatility, currency fluctuations, interest rate changes, or credit risks. While traditional risk management strategies often rely on qualitative assessments or historical data, financial analytics offers a more data-driven approach to identifying, quantifying, and mitigating risks. One of the primary benefits of using analytics for risk management is the ability to detect patterns and anomalies that may signal potential risks. For example, by analyzing transaction data, a business might identify unusual activity that could indicate fraud or other financial threats. Similarly, analytics can be used to monitor changes in market conditions or economic indicators that could impact a company's financial performance. In addition to detecting risks, analytics can also be used to quantify the potential impact of various risks on a business's financial health.

For example, a company might use value-at-risk (VaR) models to estimate the potential loss it could incur due to market fluctuations. By understanding the potential impact of these risks, businesses can develop strategies to mitigate them, such as diversifying investments, hedging currency exposure, or adjusting pricing strategies. Moreover, financial analytics allows businesses to stress-test their financial models by simulating worst-case scenarios. For example, a company might simulate the impact of a severe economic downturn or a sudden increase in interest rates on its cash flow, profitability, and liquidity. By analyzing these stress tests, businesses can identify weaknesses in their financial strategy and develop contingency plans to address potential risks.

Optimizing Investments and Portfolio Management

Analytics is not only useful for managing day-to-day financial operations but also plays a crucial role in optimizing investments and managing portfolios. Investment decisions, whether for individual stocks, bonds, or entire portfolios, are often complex and require careful consideration of a wide range of factors. Financial analytics provides the tools needed to make more informed investment decisions and maximize returns. One of the most significant contributions of analytics to investment management is the ability to create optimized portfolios. By analyzing historical performance data, market trends, and risk factors, businesses can develop portfolios that balance risk and return according to their financial goals. For example, modern portfolio theory (MPT), which is a popular framework in finance, uses analytics to create portfolios that minimize risk for a given level of expected return. Additionally, financial analytics enables businesses to continuously monitor portfolio performance and adjust their investment strategies in response to market changes.

For example, if an investment portfolio is underperforming due to a downturn in a specific industry, analytics can help identify alternative investment opportunities that offer better returns with less risk. This dynamic approach to portfolio management allows businesses to remain agile and responsive to market conditions, ensuring that their investments continue to align with their financial objectives. Analytics also plays a critical role in asset allocation, which involves determining how to distribute investments across different asset classes, such as stocks, bonds, real estate, or commodities. By analyzing historical data and market trends, businesses can develop asset allocation strategies that maximize returns while minimizing risk. For example, a company might use analytics to determine the optimal mix of high-risk, high-reward assets and lower-risk, stable investments based on its financial goals and risk tolerance.

Enhancing Cash Flow Management

Cash flow management is one of the most critical aspects of financial success for any business. Poor cash flow management can lead to liquidity problems, missed opportunities, and even bankruptcy. Analytics provides businesses with the tools needed to gain better control over their cash flow and ensure that they have the liquidity needed to meet their financial obligations and invest in growth opportunities. One of the keyways analytics enhances cash flow management is by providing real-time visibility into cash flow performance. By analyzing transactional data, businesses can monitor cash inflows and outflows in real-time, allowing them to identify potential cash flow shortages or surpluses early. This visibility enables businesses to take proactive measures, such as securing additional financing, delaying discretionary spending, or accelerating accounts receivable collection to maintain healthy cash flow levels. In addition to real-time monitoring, financial analytics can also be used to forecast future cash flow based on historical data and market conditions. For example, a business might use predictive analytics to forecast how changes in customer demand, pricing strategies, or operational costs will impact future cash flow. By developing accurate cash flow forecasts, businesses can plan for future investments, manage debt, and avoid liquidity crises.

Another critical aspect of cash flow management is working capital optimization. Working capital refers to the difference between a company's current assets, such as cash and accounts receivable, and its current liabilities, such as accounts payable and short-term debt. Analytics can help businesses optimize their working capital by analyzing factors such as payment terms, inventory turnover, and accounts receivable collection. For example, a business might use analytics to identify customers who consistently pay late and adjust payment terms or implement stricter collection practices to improve cash flow. Incorporating analytics into financial management is no longer optional for businesses aiming to achieve long-term financial success. From financial planning and forecasting to risk management and portfolio optimization, analytics provides the insights needed to make more informed, strategic decisions. By leveraging data-driven insights, businesses can not only enhance their financial performance but also gain a competitive edge in today's fast-paced, data-driven world. Financial analytics is more than just a tool for crunching numbers—it's a strategic asset that enables businesses to navigate the complexities of the financial landscape with confidence. Whether it's forecasting revenue, optimizing investments, or managing cash flow, businesses that embrace analytics are better equipped to achieve their financial goals and drive sustainable growth.

CHAPTER 4

Driving Marketing Success with Analytics

Marketing has always been an essential component of business success. However, as digital channels continue to grow, consumer behavior evolves, and competition intensifies, traditional marketing strategies are no longer enough to guarantee success. Today's marketers need data-driven insights to develop effective campaigns, engage with their target audiences, and optimize their marketing efforts. This is where analytics comes into play. Analytical research has revolutionized the way businesses approach marketing, allowing them to move away from guesswork and assumptions to make informed, data-backed decisions that drive results. This chapter explores how analytics transforms marketing, from understanding audience behavior to optimizing campaigns and measuring return on investment (ROI). We will examine the tools, techniques, and processes involved in using analytics to create marketing strategies that lead to success in today's competitive landscape.

Understanding Audience Behavior with Analytics

One of the most powerful applications of analytics in marketing is its ability to provide deep insights into audience behavior. By analyzing data from various sources—such as website visits, social media interactions, and purchasing patterns—marketers can develop a comprehensive understanding of their customers' preferences, interests, and needs. This information is critical for creating targeted, personalized marketing campaigns that resonate with specific audience segments. In the past, marketers relied heavily on demographic data, such as age, gender, and location, to define their target audiences. While this information is still important, it is no longer sufficient. With the rise of digital marketing channels, audience behavior has become more complex, and marketers need to go beyond basic demographics to truly understand their customers. For example, analytics can provide insights into how customers interact with a brand across different digital touchpoints, such as social media platforms, websites, and email campaigns. By tracking user behavior, marketers can identify patterns, such as which pages customers visit most frequently, how long they stay on a website, or which products they add to their carts but don't purchase. This level of detail allows marketers to create highly personalized campaigns that speak directly to the customer's interests and pain points.

Segmenting Audiences for Personalized Marketing

One of the key benefits of using analytics in marketing is the ability to segment audiences based on various factors, such as behavior, preferences, or purchasing history. Segmentation allows marketers to create targeted campaigns for specific groups of customers, increasing the likelihood of engagement and conversion.

There are several ways to segment audiences using analytics:

Behavioral Segmentation: This approach involves grouping customers based on their behavior, such as how they interact with a website, how often they purchase products, or their preferred communication channels. For example, an eCommerce business might segment customers into "frequent buyers" and "one-time purchasers," allowing them to tailor their marketing messages accordingly.

Demographic Segmentation: While basic, demographic segmentation is still useful for creating general audience profiles. Analytics can help refine these profiles by providing more detailed demographic data, such as income level, occupation, or educational background, which can inform campaign messaging and positioning.

Geographic Segmentation: Analytics can also be used to segment audiences based on their geographic location. This is particularly useful for businesses with location-based services or products. For instance, a restaurant chain might use geographic data to target customers within a specific radius of their locations with special promotions or discounts.

Psychographic Segmentation: This type of segmentation goes deeper by analyzing customers' values, interests, and lifestyle choices. Psychographic data provides insights into what motivates customers to make purchasing decisions, allowing marketers to create messaging that resonates on a personal level.

Optimizing Campaigns with Real-Time Data

One of the most significant advantages of using analytics in marketing is the ability to optimize campaigns in real time. In the past, marketers had to wait until the end of a campaign to assess its effectiveness and make adjustments. Today, analytics tools allow marketers to track campaign performance in real time, providing immediate feedback on what's working and what's not. For example, marketers can use analytics to monitor key performance indicators (KPIs) such as click-through rates (CTR), conversion rates, and cost-per-click (CPC) for digital advertising campaigns. If a campaign is underperforming, marketers can quickly identify the issue—whether it's the targeting, creative content, or bidding strategy—and make adjustments to improve performance. This level of agility is critical in today's fast-paced marketing environment, where trends and consumer behavior can change rapidly. In addition to optimizing digital advertising campaigns, analytics can also be used to improve other aspects of marketing, such as content marketing and email campaigns. For instance, by analyzing engagement metrics such as open rates, click rates, and time spent on content, marketers can identify which topics resonate most with their audience and adjust their content strategy accordingly. Similarly, email marketers can use analytics to test different subject lines, email designs, and messaging to determine which combinations lead to higher open and conversion rates.

A/B Testing and Experimentation

A/B testing, also known as split testing, is a critical technique used in marketing analytics to compare two or more versions of a marketing asset to determine which performs better. A/B testing is often used to test variations of digital ads, email campaigns, landing pages, and website elements. By analyzing the results of these tests, marketers can identify which version of the asset is more effective in driving conversions, engagement, or other desired outcomes. For example, an eCommerce company might run an A/B test to compare two different product landing page designs. Version A could feature a larger product image and a "Buy Now" button, while Version B might have a different layout with more detailed product descriptions. By analyzing metrics such as conversion rates, bounce rates, and time spent on the page, the company can determine which design leads to more sales and use that version for future campaigns. A/B testing is an essential tool for optimizing marketing efforts because it allows marketers to make data-driven decisions based on actual customer behavior rather than assumptions or preferences. By continually experimenting and testing different elements of their campaigns, marketers can improve performance and drive better results over time.

Measuring Marketing ROI with Analytics

One of the most challenging aspects of marketing is measuring return on investment (ROI). Marketing efforts often span multiple channels and touchpoints, making it difficult to determine which activities are contributing to revenue and business growth. However, analytics provides the tools needed to measure marketing ROI accurately and demonstrate the value of marketing investments. Marketing analytics enables businesses to track every interaction a customer has with a brand, from the first point of contact to the final purchase. By analyzing this data, marketers can determine the effectiveness of each marketing channel and campaign in driving conversions and generating revenue. For example, a business might use attribution modeling to assign credit to different touchpoints along the customer journey. Attribution models help marketers understand how different marketing efforts—such as paid search, social media ads, email campaigns, or content marketing—contribute to a customer's decision to make a purchase. By identifying the most effective touchpoints, businesses can allocate their marketing budgets more effectively and invest in the channels that deliver the highest ROI. In addition to tracking revenue, analytics can also be used to measure other aspects of marketing success, such as customer lifetime value (CLV) and customer acquisition cost (CAC). CLV represents the total revenue a business can expect to generate from a customer over their entire relationship with the brand, while CAC represents the cost of acquiring a new customer. By comparing CLV to CAC, businesses can assess the profitability of their marketing efforts and make data-driven decisions about how to optimize customer acquisition strategies.

Predictive Analytics for Future Marketing Trends

While descriptive analytics helps marketers understand what has happened in the past, predictive analytics allows them to anticipate future trends and make proactive decisions. Predictive analytics uses historical data, machine learning algorithms, and statistical models to forecast future outcomes, such as customer behavior, market demand, or campaign performance.

In marketing, predictive analytics can be used to:

Forecast Customer Behavior: By analyzing past purchase data, browsing behavior, and engagement metrics, predictive models can identify which customers are most likely to make a purchase or churn. Marketers can use this information to create targeted retention campaigns or cross-sell offers for high-value customers.

Optimize Campaign Timing: Predictive analytics can help marketers determine the best times to launch campaigns based on historical data. For example, an online retailer might use predictive models to forecast peak shopping periods and schedule promotions accordingly to maximize sales.

Identify Emerging Trends: Predictive analytics can analyze market trends, social media conversations, and industry data to identify emerging consumer preferences or new product opportunities. This foresight enables marketers to stay ahead of the competition and capitalize on new trends before they become mainstream.

Personalize Marketing at Scale: Predictive models can be used to personalize marketing messages at scale. For instance, an eCommerce business might use predictive analytics to recommend products to customers based on their browsing and purchase history, increasing the likelihood of conversion.

Marketing success in today's digital age requires more than creativity and intuition requires data-driven insights and a commitment to ongoing optimization. Analytics provides the tools marketers need to understand their audiences, create personalized campaigns, and measure the impact of their efforts. From audience segmentation and campaign optimization to predictive analytics and ROI measurement, analytics plays a critical role in driving marketing success. As businesses continue to collect and analyze more data, the ability to leverage marketing analytics will become even more important. By integrating analytics into their marketing strategies, businesses can create more effective campaigns, improve customer engagement, and ultimately drive long-term growth.

CHAPTER 5

Analytics In Project Planning and Launches

Project planning and execution have always been critical to business success, but in today's fast-paced, data-driven world, relying solely on traditional project management methods is no longer sufficient. Analytics has become an essential tool in ensuring that projects are not only delivered on time and within budget but also meet their strategic goals. From the initial planning stages to post-launch analysis, data can provide valuable insights that enhance decision-making, resource allocation, risk management, and overall project performance. This chapter explores how analytics can be leveraged throughout the entire lifecycle of a project, from the initial planning stages to the launch and beyond. We will discuss how businesses can use data to predict project success, allocate resources efficiently, manage timelines, and measure outcomes. By the end of this chapter, you'll understand how to integrate analytics into your project management processes to improve outcomes and ensure successful project launches.

Using Data for Project Planning

The planning phase of any project sets the foundation for success. A well-thought-out plan considers objectives, timelines, resources, risks, and stakeholders. However, the complexity of modern projects, combined with ever-changing market conditions, means that plans based purely on assumptions or historical data may fall short. Analytics provides a more dynamic approach to project planning by offering real-time data, predictive insights, and scenario modeling. One of the most significant advantages of using analytics in project planning is its ability to forecast potential outcomes. Predictive analytics can use historical project data, combined with external factors such as market conditions, industry trends, or resource availability, to estimate the likelihood of project success. This allows project managers to make informed decisions about whether to proceed with a project, how to allocate resources, and how to set realistic timelines.

For example, a construction company might use predictive analytics to assess whether a new building project will be completed on time and within budget. By analyzing past projects of similar scope, the company can identify potential risks—such as supply chain delays or cost overruns—and adjust the project plan accordingly. This proactive approach minimizes the likelihood of surprises during the execution phase and ensures that the project remains on track. In addition to predictive analytics, descriptive analytics plays a critical role in project planning by providing insights into past project performance. By analyzing historical data, project managers can identify patterns or trends that may impact future projects. For instance, if past projects consistently experienced delays during a specific phase, analytics can help identify the root cause, whether it's resource shortages, miscommunication, or unforeseen external factors. Armed with this information, project managers can take steps to mitigate these issues in future projects.

Resource Allocation and Optimization

Efficient resource allocation is one of the most challenging aspects of project management. Allocating too many resources to a project can lead to inefficiencies and increased costs, while allocating too few can result in delays, missed deadlines, or poor-quality work. Analytics provides project managers with the data they need to optimize resource allocation and ensure that each project has the right mix of personnel, materials, and time to succeed. Resource analytics involves analyzing data on available resources—such as staff, equipment, and materials—and matching them to the needs of the project. For example, a software development company might use resource analytics to determine how many developers, designers, and testers are needed for a new app launch. By analyzing past projects, the company can identify the optimal team size and skill mix required to meet the project's goals.

One of the key benefits of using analytics for resource allocation is the ability to identify potential bottlenecks before they occur. For example, if a company has multiple projects running simultaneously, analytics can help identify resource conflicts, such as a shortage of skilled personnel or limited access to critical equipment. By identifying these bottlenecks early, project managers can reallocate resources or adjust timelines to avoid delays and ensure that all projects remain on schedule. Additionally, analytics can be used to track resource utilization throughout the lifecycle of the project. This allows project managers to monitor whether resources are being used efficiently or if adjustments need to be made. For instance, if a team is consistently underperforming or facing roadblocks, analytics can provide insights into whether the issue is related to staffing, equipment availability, or process inefficiencies. By making data-driven adjustments, project managers can optimize resource use and keep the project on track.

Timeline Management and Milestone Tracking

One of the most significant challenges in project management is ensuring that projects are completed on time. Delays can have a ripple effect, impacting not only the project itself but also other initiatives, budgets, and customer satisfaction. Analytics plays a critical role in timeline management by providing project managers with real-time data on project progress, potential delays, and overall performance. Predictive analytics can be particularly useful in timeline management by forecasting how long specific tasks or phases of a project will take. By analyzing past data on similar projects, predictive models can estimate the duration of each phase, taking into account factors such as team performance, external dependencies, and resource availability. This allows project managers to set more accurate timelines and avoid unrealistic deadlines that lead to delays and cost overruns. In addition to predictive models, descriptive analytics can be used to monitor the progress of a project in real time.

By tracking key performance indicators (KPIs), such as task completion rates, hours worked, and budget utilization, project managers can quickly identify whether the project is on track or if adjustments need to be made. For example, if a project is consistently falling behind schedule, analytics can help pinpoint the cause—whether it's due to underperformance, resource shortages, or external factors—and provide data-driven recommendations for getting the project back on track. One of the most valuable features of analytics in project management is the ability to set and track milestones. Milestones are critical checkpoints in a project that indicate whether key deliverables have been met. By using analytics to monitor milestone completion, project managers can ensure that the project is progressing as planned and identify potential issues early. For example, if a critical milestone is missed, analytics can help determine whether the delay is due to poor resource allocation, timeline mismanagement, or external factors. This enables project managers to take corrective action before the project falls too far behind.

Risk Management and Mitigation

Every project carries a certain level of risk, whether it's financial, operational, or strategic. One of the key benefits of using analytics in project management is its ability to identify and mitigate risks before they become critical issues. By analyzing data from past projects, external factors, and real-time performance metrics, project managers can proactively address potential risks and ensure that the project remains on track. One of the primary tools used in risk management is risk modeling. Risk models use historical data and statistical techniques to estimate the likelihood of specific risks occurring and the potential impact they will have on the project. For example, a company planning a new product launch might use a risk model to assess the likelihood of supply chain disruptions, cost overruns, or regulatory delays. By understanding the probability and impact of these risks, the company can develop contingency plans and adjust its project plan accordingly. In addition to risk modeling, real-time risk monitoring plays a critical role in managing project risks. By tracking performance metrics—such as budget utilization, task completion rates, or resource availability—project managers can quickly identify when a project is veering off course and take corrective action.

For instance, if a project is consistently exceeding its budget, analytics can help identify whether the issue is due to poor resource allocation, scope creep, or other factors. By addressing the root cause of the problem early, project managers can prevent further cost overruns and ensure that the project remains within budget. Another critical aspect of risk management is scenario analysis. Scenario analysis allows project managers to model different potential outcomes based on various risk factors. For example, a company might simulate the impact of a supplier delay or a change in market conditions on the overall project timeline. By analyzing these scenarios, project managers can develop strategies to mitigate risks, such as securing alternative suppliers, adjusting timelines, or reallocating resources.

Post-Launch Analytics and Performance Measurement

The role of analytics in project management doesn't end with the successful completion of the project. Once a project has been launched, it's essential to analyze its performance to determine whether it meets its objectives, identify areas for improvement, and gather insights for future projects. Post-launch analytics involves collecting and analyzing data on key performance indicators (KPIs), such as project outcomes, customer feedback, financial performance, and operational efficiency. One of the most critical aspects of post-launch analytics is measuring project success. Success can be defined in various ways, depending on the goals of the project. For example, a software development project might measure success based on user adoption rates, customer satisfaction, or revenue generated. By analyzing these KPIs, project managers can assess whether the project delivered the desired outcomes and identify areas for improvement in future projects. In addition to measuring success, post-launch analytics also plays a crucial role in continuous improvement. By analyzing data from past projects, businesses can identify patterns or trends that lead to successful outcomes or common pitfalls that lead to project failure. For instance, if multiple projects consistently experience delays during a specific phase, analytics can help identify the root cause and provide recommendations for improving future project timelines.

Another critical aspect of post-launch analytics is financial analysis. By comparing the project's actual costs to its projected budget, businesses can assess whether the project was completed within budget or if there were cost overruns. This analysis can also provide insights into resource utilization, operational efficiency, and overall project ROI. By understanding the financial performance of a project, businesses can make more informed decisions about future investments and resource allocation. Analytics has become an indispensable tool in project management, from the initial planning stages to post-launch performance measurement. By leveraging data, businesses can optimize resource allocation, manage timelines, mitigate risks, and ensure successful project outcomes. Whether it's predicting project success, tracking milestone completion, or measuring ROI, analytics provides the insights needed to improve project performance and achieve long-term success. As businesses continue to adopt data-driven approaches to project management, the ability to use analytics effectively will become increasingly important. By integrating analytics into their project planning and execution processes, businesses can enhance decision-making, reduce risks, and ensure that projects are delivered on time, within budget, and with the desired outcomes.

CHAPTER 6

Building A Data-Driven Culture

A data-driven culture is one in which decision-making processes at every level of the organization are guided by data and analytical insights. In today's business environment, the ability to integrate data into the fabric of a company's operations can differentiate successful organizations from those that lag behind. While many businesses have adopted analytics tools and technologies, the true power of analytics can only be realized when data becomes an integral part of the organizational mindset and culture. Building a data-driven culture requires more than simply investing in technology or hiring data experts; it requires a shift in thinking, processes, and behavior across all departments and roles. This chapter explores the importance of creating a data-driven culture, the steps necessary to cultivate such a culture, and the challenges organizations may face during the transition. By the end of this chapter, you'll have a clearer understanding of how to embed data-driven decision-making into the core of your organization, leading to more effective strategies, improved performance, and long-term growth.

Why a Data-Driven Culture Matters

Organizations that embrace a data-driven culture gain numerous benefits, including improved decision-making, increased efficiency, enhanced innovation, and stronger competitive advantage. When data is used consistently and effectively across all levels of the organization, it creates a foundation for informed decisions that are based on evidence rather than intuition or assumptions. In traditional organizations, decisions are often made based on experience, hierarchy, or opinion. While these factors are still valuable, relying solely on them can lead to bias, missed opportunities, and suboptimal outcomes. In contrast, a data-driven culture encourages teams to seek out data before making decisions, reducing the likelihood of errors and improving the overall quality of decision-making. Additionally, a data-driven culture fosters transparency and accountability. When decisions are backed by data, it becomes easier to track progress, measure outcomes, and hold individuals or teams accountable for their results. This level of transparency helps create a culture of continuous improvement, where teams are constantly looking for ways to optimize their performance based on real-time insights.

The Building Blocks of a Data-Driven Culture

Creating a data-driven culture involves a series of steps that organizations must take to ensure that data is integrated into every aspect of their operations. These steps include fostering leadership buy-in, democratizing data access, developing data literacy, and encouraging collaboration across departments.

Leadership Buy-In: The journey toward a data-driven culture begins at the top. Leadership buy-in is essential for creating a culture that prioritizes data-driven decision-making. When leaders actively promote and model the use of data in their decision-making processes, it sets a precedent for the rest of the organization. Leaders play a critical role in shaping organizational culture, and their attitudes toward data can influence how other employees perceive its importance. For instance, if a CEO or senior manager emphasizes the value of data in strategic planning meetings, other employees are more likely to follow suit and incorporate data into their own work. In addition to promoting the use of data, leaders must also provide the necessary resources and support for building a data-driven culture. This may include investing in analytics tools, hiring data experts, and providing training opportunities to help employees develop their data skills. Without leadership support, efforts to build a data-driven culture are likely to falter.

Democratizing Data Access: One of the key principles of a data-driven culture is that data should be accessible to everyone in the organization, not just data scientists or IT professionals. Democratizing data access means ensuring that employees at all levels and in all departments have the ability to access, analyze, and use data in their daily work. In many organizations, data is siloed within specific departments or systems, making it difficult for employees outside of those areas to access the information they need. To overcome this challenge, organizations must invest in data management systems that allow for seamless data sharing and collaboration across teams. This might involve implementing cloud-based data platforms, creating centralized data repositories, or using tools that allow employees to visualize and analyze data without requiring advanced technical skills. By democratizing data access, organizations empower employees to take ownership of their decisions and contribute to the overall success of the business. When everyone has the tools and information they need to make data-driven decisions, it leads to more efficient processes, better outcomes, and a more agile organization.

Developing Data Literacy: While democratizing data access is important, it's not enough on its own. Employees must also have the skills and knowledge to interpret and use data effectively. This is where data literacy comes into play. Data literacy refers to the ability to read, understand, and communicate data in a meaningful way. In a data-driven culture, all employees, not just data specialists, should be equipped with the skills to analyze data, draw insights, and use those insights to inform their decisions. Developing data literacy across the organization is critical to ensuring that data-driven decision-making becomes the norm rather than the exception. Organizations can develop data literacy through a combination of formal training programs, on-the-job learning, and mentorship. For example, companies might offer workshops or online courses that teach employees how to use analytics tools, interpret data visualizations, or conduct basic statistical analyses. Additionally, pairing data experts with employees from non-technical backgrounds can help bridge the gap between data science and business operations, ensuring that data insights are translated into actionable strategies. It's important to recognize that developing data literacy is an ongoing process.

Encouraging Cross Departmental Collaboration

A data-driven culture thrives on collaboration, particularly when it comes to sharing data and insights across departments. In many organizations, data silos prevent teams from fully leveraging the power of data. For example, the marketing team may have valuable customer data that could benefit the sales or product development teams, but if this data isn't shared, opportunities are missed. To build a truly data-driven culture, organizations must break down these silos and encourage cross-departmental collaboration. This can be achieved through a combination of technology and processes that facilitate data sharing. For instance, cloud-based data platforms allow teams to access and analyze data in real time, regardless of their location or department. Additionally, creating cross-functional teams that include representatives from different departments can help ensure that data insights are shared and used across the organization. Collaboration doesn't just apply to sharing data; it also involves working together to develop data-driven strategies. By bringing together employees with diverse perspectives and expertise, organizations can create more innovative and effective solutions to business challenges. For example, a cross-functional team might work together to analyze customer data, identify trends, and develop a new product offering that meets emerging consumer needs.

Overcoming Challenges in Building a Data-Driven Culture

While the benefits of a data-driven culture are clear, building such a culture is not without its challenges. Organizations often encounter resistance to change, data quality issues, and a lack of alignment between data initiatives and business objectives. By anticipating these challenges and developing strategies to address them, organizations can successfully transition to a data-driven culture.

Resistance to Change: One of the most common challenges organizations face when building a data-driven culture is resistance to change. Employees may be hesitant to adopt new tools or processes, particularly if they are used to relying on intuition or experience to make decisions. This resistance can be particularly strong in organizations with a long history of traditional decision-making practices. To overcome resistance to change, organizations must focus on creating a culture of trust and transparency. Leaders should clearly communicate the benefits of data-driven decision-making and demonstrate how it can lead to better outcomes for both the organization and individual employees. Additionally, providing training and support can help employees feel more comfortable using data in their work. It's also important to recognize that building a data-driven culture is a gradual process. Organizations should start by implementing small, data-driven initiatives and gradually expand as employees become more familiar with using data. Over time, as employees see the positive impact of data-driven decision-making, resistance to change is likely to diminish.

Ensuring Data Quality: Data quality is a critical factor in building a data-driven culture. If employees do not trust the accuracy or reliability of the data they are using, they are unlikely to incorporate it into their decision-making processes. Ensuring data quality involves implementing robust data governance practices, such as data cleaning, validation, and auditing, to ensure that data is accurate, consistent, and up to date. Organizations should also focus on creating clear guidelines for data entry and management. For example, establishing standardized procedures for collecting and storing data can help prevent errors and inconsistencies. Additionally, regular audits of data systems can identify any issues with data quality and ensure that they are addressed promptly.

Aligning Data Initiatives with Business Objectives

Another challenge in building a data-driven culture is ensuring that data initiatives are aligned with the organization's overall business objectives. In some cases, data projects may be pursued without a clear understanding of how they will contribute to the organization's strategic goals. This can lead to wasted resources and a lack of buy-in from employees. To avoid this issue, organizations should develop a clear data strategy that outlines how data initiatives will support business objectives. This strategy should be communicated to all employees, ensuring that everyone understands the role data plays in achieving the organization's goals. Additionally, regular reviews of data projects can help ensure that they remain aligned with business objectives and deliver measurable value. Building a data-driven culture is essential for organizations looking to thrive in today's competitive, data-centric world. By fostering leadership buy-in, democratizing data access, developing data literacy, and encouraging cross-departmental collaboration, businesses can embed data-driven decision-making into their core operations. While challenges such as resistance to change, data quality issues, and misalignment between data initiatives and business objectives may arise, these can be overcome with the right strategies and a commitment to continuous improvement.

CHAPTER 7

Tools and Techniques for Effective Analytics

The world of data analytics is vast, encompassing a wide array of tools and techniques designed to help businesses gather, process, and interpret data. These tools allow organizations to unlock valuable insights, optimize operations, enhance customer experiences, and drive strategic decision-making. However, with so many tools and methodologies available, it can be overwhelming to determine which ones are best suited to specific business needs. In this chapter, we'll explore the most effective tools and techniques used in analytics, focusing on how businesses can choose the right ones for their unique goals. From data collection and storage to advanced analytics techniques like machine learning, predictive analytics, and data visualization, this chapter will provide you with the knowledge you need to implement effective analytics within your organization.

Data Collection and Storage Tools

Before any meaningful analysis can occur, data must be collected and stored efficiently. Data collection involves gathering information from various sources, including customer interactions, business transactions, sensor data, and more. Once collected, data needs to be stored in a way that allows easy access and processing.

Data Collection Tools

Data collection is the first step in any analytics process, and businesses have a wide range of tools at their disposal for gathering data:

Customer Relationship Management (CRM) Systems: CRM tools like Salesforce, HubSpot, and Zoho CRM are widely used to collect and store customer data, such as contact information, purchase history, and interaction details. This data is essential for customer segmentation, personalization, and marketing efforts.

Web Analytics Tools: Tools like Google Analytics, Adobe Analytics, and Hotjar are commonly used to track website traffic, user behavior, and engagement metrics. These tools provide insights into how visitors interact with a website, helping businesses optimize their online presence and improve conversion rates.

Social media Analytics Tools: Platforms like Sprout Social, Hootsuite, and Buffer allow businesses to collect data from social media platforms, including engagement metrics, follower demographics, and sentiment analysis. This data is crucial for developing targeted social media marketing campaigns.

Survey Tools: Tools like SurveyMonkey, Google Forms, and Type form are used to collect primary data directly from customers or employees through surveys and questionnaires. This method is especially useful for gathering customer feedback, employee engagement data, or market research insights.

IoT Devices and Sensors: For businesses that rely on physical products or services, Internet of Things (IoT) devices and sensors can be used to collect data on everything from equipment performance to environmental conditions. This data is crucial for predictive maintenance, supply chain optimization, and process automation.

Data Storage Solutions

Once data is collected, it needs to be stored in a way that allows for easy access, analysis, and scalability. Modern businesses rely on a variety of data storage solutions, depending on their size, industry, and specific needs:

Relational Databases: Relational databases, such as MySQL, PostgreSQL, and Microsoft SQL Server, are commonly used to store structured data. These databases organize data into tables with predefined relationships, making it easy to query and analyze using SQL (Structured Query Language).

Data Warehouses: For larger organizations with massive amounts of data, data warehouses like Amazon Redshift, Google BigQuery, and Snowflake provide centralized storage for both structured and unstructured data. Data warehouses are designed to handle large-scale analytics, allowing businesses to run complex queries across vast data sets.

Cloud Storage: Cloud-based storage solutions like Amazon S3, Google Cloud Storage, and Microsoft Azure allow businesses to store data remotely, ensuring scalability and flexibility. Cloud storage is particularly useful for businesses that need to access and analyze data from multiple locations or devices.

Data Lakes: Unlike traditional databases, data lakes store raw, unstructured data in their native format. Tools like Hadoop and AWS Lake Formation are often used to build data lakes, which are ideal for organizations that need to store large volumes of diverse data types for future analysis.

Data Processing and Cleaning Tools

Once data is collected and stored, it often requires processing and cleaning before analysis can take place. Data processing involves transforming raw data into a usable format, while data cleaning ensures that the data is accurate, complete, and free of errors.

Data Cleaning Tools

Data cleaning is a critical step in the analytics process, as dirty or incomplete data can lead to inaccurate insights and flawed decision-making. Fortunately, several tools are available to automate and streamline the data cleaning process:

Trifacta: Trifacta is a popular tool that helps organizations clean and prepare data for analysis. It uses machine learning to detect and correct data quality issues, such as missing values, duplicates, and formatting errors.

Open Refine: Open Refine is an open-source data cleaning tool that allows users to explore large datasets, clean inconsistencies, and transform data into structured formats. It is particularly useful for cleaning unstructured data or dealing with messy datasets.

Talend: Talend is a comprehensive data integration and management tool that includes features for data cleaning, transformation, and preparation. It supports various data sources and formats, making it a versatile choice for businesses with diverse data needs.

Alteryx: Alteryx is a powerful data preparation tool that allows users to clean, blend, and transform data through a user-friendly interface. It is commonly used for automating data workflows and preparing data for advanced analytics.

Data Processing Tools

Data processing involves transforming raw data into formats that are suitable for analysis. This can include aggregating data, calculating statistics, or applying transformations to normalize or standardize data. Several tools are available for data processing:

Apache Spark: Apache Spark is an open-source data processing engine that can handle large-scale data processing tasks across distributed systems. It is widely used for processing both batch and real-time data and is a popular choice for big data analytics.

ETL (Extract, Transform, Load) Tools: ETL tools like Informatica, Apache NiFi, and Fivetran are designed to extract data from various sources, transform it into a suitable format, and load it into a target system for analysis. These tools are essential for integrating data from multiple sources and ensuring that they are ready for analysis.

Python and R: For more hands-on data processing, programming languages like Python and R are widely used by data scientists and analysts. Libraries such as Pandas (Python) and Dplyr (R) allow users to manipulate and process large datasets with ease.

Advanced Analytics Techniques

Once data has been collected, cleaned, and processed, businesses can apply a variety of advanced analytics techniques to extract insights and inform decision-making. These techniques range from basic statistical analysis to more complex machine learning algorithms and predictive modeling.

Descriptive Analytics

Descriptive analytics is the most basic form of analytics and involves summarizing historical data to understand what has happened in the past. It focuses on providing insights into trends, patterns, and key metrics that can help businesses understand their performance.

Dashboards: Tools like Tableau, Power BI, and Qlik Sense are commonly used to create interactive dashboards that visualize historical data. These dashboards allow businesses to track key performance indicators (KPIs) and identify trends over time.

Reporting Tools: Reporting tools like Crystal Reports and Zoho Analytics are used to generate detailed reports based on historical data. These reports can be customized to provide insights into specific business functions, such as sales performance, customer behavior, or operational efficiency.

Predictive Analytics

Predictive analytics goes beyond historical analysis and uses data to forecast future outcomes. This type of analytics relies on statistical models, machine learning algorithms, and pattern recognition to predict what is likely to happen based on historical data.

Regression Analysis: Regression analysis is a statistical technique used to model the relationship between variables. It is commonly used in predictive analytics to forecast outcomes based on historical trends. For example, businesses might use regression analysis to predict sales revenue based on past sales performance and market conditions.

Time Series Analysis: Time series analysis involves analyzing data points collected over time to identify patterns and forecast future trends. This technique is widely used in finance, supply chain management, and demand forecasting.

Machine Learning: Machine learning algorithms, such as decision trees, random forests, and neural networks, are increasingly used in predictive analytics. These algorithms can automatically learn from historical data to make accurate predictions about future outcomes. For instance, eCommerce companies use machine learning to recommend products based on customers' browsing and purchasing history.

Predictive Modeling Tools: Tools like SAS, IBM Watson, and Data Robot offer comprehensive platforms for building predictive models. These tools allow businesses to apply machine learning algorithms to large datasets and generate forecasts for various business scenarios.

Prescriptive Analytics

While predictive analytics focuses on forecasting future outcomes, prescriptive analytics goes a step further by providing recommendations on how to achieve desired outcomes. It combines data, models, and algorithms to suggest the best course of action for a given situation.

Optimization Algorithms: Prescriptive analytics often relies on optimization algorithms, such as linear programming or genetic algorithms, to find the most efficient solution to a problem. For example, a company might use optimization algorithms to minimize production costs while maximizing output.

Decision Management Tools: Tools like IBM Decision Optimization and Gurobi are commonly used for prescriptive analytics. These tools help businesses model complex scenarios and make data-driven decisions based on real-time data and predictive insights.

Data Visualization and Interpretation

Data visualization is a critical component of effective analytics, as it allows businesses to interpret and communicate complex data in a clear and understandable way. Visualization tools transform raw data into charts, graphs, maps, and other visual representations that make it easier to identify trends, patterns, and outliers.

Data Visualization Tools

Tableau: Tableau is one of the most popular data visualization tools on the market, offering a user-friendly interface and a wide range of visualization options. It allows users to create interactive dashboards, charts, and maps that can be shared across teams for collaborative decision-making.

Power BI: Power BI, developed by Microsoft, is another powerful data visualization tool that integrates seamlessly with other Microsoft products like Excel and Azure. It is commonly used for creating interactive reports and dashboards that provide real-time insights into business performance.

D3.js: For more customized visualizations, D3.js is a JavaScript library that allows developers to create highly interactive and customizable data visualizations for web-based applications. While it requires coding skills, D3.js offers unparalleled flexibility in designing visualizations.

Google Data Studio: Google Data Studio is a free data visualization tool that allows users to create interactive reports and dashboards using data from Google Analytics, Google Ads, and other data sources. It is ideal for businesses that rely heavily on Google's ecosystem of products.

Effective analytics relies on the right combination of tools and techniques. From data collection and storage to advanced analytics techniques like machine learning and predictive modeling, businesses have a wide array of options to choose from. The key to success is selecting the tools and methodologies that align with your business goals, ensuring that data is processed accurately, and leveraging the right analytics techniques to extract meaningful insights. As the world of analytics continues to evolve, businesses that invest in the right tools and techniques will be well-positioned to stay ahead of the competition and drive strategic decision-making. Whether you are just starting on your analytics journey or looking to enhance your existing capabilities, the tools and techniques outlined in this chapter will provide a strong foundation for achieving success with data-driven decision-making.

CHAPTER 8

Predictive Analytics and Forecasting

In a world where businesses are constantly seeking ways to gain a competitive edge, predictive analytics and forecasting have become essential tools. Predictive analytics takes historical data and uses statistical models and machine learning algorithms to predict future outcomes, while forecasting applies this data to estimate what's likely to happen in a specific time frame. Together, they offer businesses the ability to anticipate future trends, optimize decision-making, and reduce uncertainty. Predictive analytics and forecasting have applications in virtually every industry, from finance and marketing to healthcare and supply chain management. This chapter will explore the key concepts behind predictive analytics, the techniques used to make accurate forecasts, and how businesses can leverage these tools to drive strategic decision-making.

The Fundamentals of Predictive Analytics

At its core, predictive analytics involves analyzing historical data to predict future outcomes. This type of analysis goes beyond traditional descriptive analytics, which only focuses on what happened in the past.

Instead, predictive analytics uses statistical models, algorithms, and machine learning techniques to anticipate future events and behaviors. Predictive analytics can be applied to a wide range of business scenarios, including forecasting sales revenue, predicting customer churn, assessing risk, and optimizing marketing campaigns. For example, an eCommerce company might use predictive analytics to identify which customers are most likely to make a purchase in the next month based on their past behavior. By anticipating customer actions, the company can target those customers with personalized offers or promotions, increasing the likelihood of conversion.

The process of predictive analytics typically involves the following steps:

Data Collection: The first step in predictive analytics is gathering relevant data. This data can come from a variety of sources, including customer transactions, website interactions, social media posts, and internal business systems. The quality and completeness of the data are critical to the accuracy of the predictions.

Data Cleaning and Preparation: Once the data is collected, it must be cleaned and prepared for analysis. This involves removing any errors, duplicates, or inconsistencies in the data. In some cases, it may also involve transforming the data into a format that can be easily analyzed by machine learning algorithms.

Model Building: After the data is prepared, analysts use statistical models or machine learning algorithms to create a predictive model. This model is trained using historical data to learn patterns and relationships that can be used to make predictions about future outcomes.

Model Validation: Before a predictive model can be used for decision-making, it must be validated to ensure its accuracy. This involves testing the model on a separate set of data (known as a validation set) to see how well it predicts outcomes. If the model performs well, it can be deployed for use in forecasting.

Prediction and Forecasting: Once the model is validated, it can be used to make predictions about future outcomes. These predictions can be used to inform business decisions, such as when to launch a new product, how to allocate resources, or which customers to target with marketing campaigns.

Techniques in Predictive Analytics

Several techniques are commonly used in predictive analytics, ranging from simple statistical methods to more complex machine learning algorithms. The choice of technique depends on the nature of the data, the business problem being addressed, and the desired level of accuracy.

Regression Analysis

Regression analysis is one of the most widely used techniques in predictive analytics. It involves modeling the relationship between a dependent variable (the outcome you want to predict) and one or more independent variables (the factors that influence the outcome). There are several types of regression analysis, including:

Linear Regression: This is the simplest form of regression analysis, where the relationship between the independent and dependent variables is assumed to be linear. For example, a company might use linear regression to predict sales revenue based on advertising spend.

Multiple Regression: Multiple regression models involve two or more independent variables. For example, a business might use multiple regression to predict customer churn based on factors such as customer satisfaction, number of purchases, and time since the last purchase.

Logistic Regression: Logistic regression is used when the dependent variable is binary (e.g., yes/no, win/lose). For example, a healthcare provider might use logistic regression to predict whether a patient will be readmitted to the hospital based on various risk factors.

Time Series Analysis

Time series analysis is a technique used to predict future outcomes based on historical data collected over time. This type of analysis is particularly useful for forecasting trends, such as sales patterns, stock prices, or weather conditions. Time series analysis accounts for the fact that data points are often dependent on previous values, allowing for more accurate predictions.

Key techniques in time series analysis include:

Moving Averages: Moving averages smooth out fluctuations in data by calculating the average of a specified number of past data points. This technique is often used to identify long-term trends in sales, stock prices, or other metrics.

Exponential Smoothing: Exponential smoothing is similar to moving averages, but it gives more weight to recent data points. This makes it more responsive to changes in the data, making it ideal for short-term forecasting.

Autoregressive Integrated Moving Average (ARIMA): ARIMA is a more complex time series model that combines autoregression, differencing, and moving averages to forecast future values. ARIMA models are widely used in finance and economics to predict stock prices, interest rates, and other time-dependent variables.

Machine Learning Algorithms

Machine learning algorithms are increasingly being used in predictive analytics due to their ability to handle large datasets and uncover complex patterns that traditional statistical methods may miss. Some of the most common machine learning techniques used in predictive analytics include:

Decision Trees: Decision trees are a popular machine learning algorithm used to classify data or predict outcomes based on a series of decisions. For example, a decision tree might be used to predict whether a customer will churn based on factors such as purchase history, satisfaction scores, and customer demographics.

Random Forest: Random forest is an extension of decision trees that uses multiple decision trees to make more accurate predictions. This technique is often used in scenarios where there are many variables that influence the outcome.

Neural Networks: Neural networks are a type of machine learning algorithm modeled after the human brain. They are particularly useful for analyzing complex, non-linear relationships in data. For example, neural networks are commonly used in image recognition, natural language processing, and customer behavior prediction.

Support Vector Machines (SVM): SVM is a supervised machine learning algorithm that is used for both classification and regression tasks. It is effective in scenarios where the relationship between the input variables and the outcome is complex and difficult to model with traditional methods.

Applications for Predictive Analytics in Business

Predictive analytics can be applied across a wide range of business functions, helping organizations make more informed decisions and achieve better outcomes. Some of the most common applications include:

Sales Forecasting: This is one of the most common use cases for predictive analytics. By analyzing historical sales data, market conditions, and external factors such as seasonality, businesses can predict future sales volumes and revenue. This allows them to allocate resources more effectively, optimize inventory levels, and plan for future growth. For example, a retail company might use predictive analytics to forecast sales for the upcoming holiday season. By analyzing past holiday sales data, customer behavior, and economic indicators, the company can estimate how much inventory stock and how to price products to maximize revenue.

Customer Behavior Prediction: Predictive analytics is widely used to anticipate customer behavior, such as predicting which customers are likely to churn, which are most likely to make a purchase, or which are likely to respond to a specific marketing campaign. By understanding customer behavior, businesses can tailor their marketing efforts to target the right customers with the right messages at the right time. For example, a subscription-based service might use predictive analytics to identify customers who are at risk of canceling their subscription. By analyzing factors such as usage patterns, customer support interactions, and payment history, the company can target those customers with retention offers or personalized outreach.

Risk Assessment and Fraud Detection: Predictive analytics is also a valuable tool for assessing risk and detecting fraud. In industries such as finance, insurance, and healthcare, businesses can use predictive models to identify high-risk customers, transactions, or claims. For example, banks use predictive analytics to detect fraudulent transactions by analyzing patterns of behavior that deviate from the norm. In insurance, predictive analytics can be used to assess the likelihood of policyholders filing claims based on their demographics, driving history, or health records. This allows insurance companies to price policies more accurately and reduce the risk of losses.

Supply Chain Optimization: Supply chain management is another area where predictive analytics can deliver significant value. By forecasting demand, businesses can optimize inventory levels, reduce costs, and improve delivery times. For example, a manufacturer might use predictive analytics to forecast demand for specific products based on historical sales data, market trends, and economic indicators. This allows them to adjust production schedules, allocate resources more efficiently, and minimize stockouts or overstock situations.

Predictive Maintenance: In industries that rely heavily on machinery and equipment, predictive maintenance is a critical application of predictive analytics. By analyzing data from sensors, maintenance logs, and machine performance, businesses can predict when equipment is likely to fail and schedule maintenance before a breakdown occurs. This approach reduces downtime, minimizes repair costs, and extends the lifespan of equipment. For example, an airline might use predictive analytics to monitor the performance of its fleet and identify potential maintenance issues before they lead to delays or safety concerns. By proactively addressing these issues, the airline can reduce operational disruptions and improve customer satisfaction.

Challenges in Implementing Predictive Analytics

While predictive analytics offers numerous benefits, it also comes with its own set of challenges. Some of the most common challenges include:

Data Quality: The accuracy of predictive models depends heavily on the quality of the data used. Incomplete, outdated, or inaccurate data can lead to flawed predictions and poor decision-making.

Data Integration: Many businesses struggle to integrate data from multiple sources, such as customer databases, financial systems, and external data providers. Without a unified data infrastructure, it can be difficult to create accurate predictive models.

Skill Gaps: Implementing predictive analytics requires specialized skills in data science, machine learning, and statistical modeling. Many businesses lack the in-house expertise to build and deploy predictive models effectively.

Interpreting Results: Even with accurate predictive models, interpreting the results and translating them into actionable insights can be challenging. Businesses need to ensure that decision-makers understand the predictions and use them to inform their strategies.

Predictive analytics and forecasting have become indispensable tools for businesses seeking to stay competitive in today's data-driven world. By leveraging historical data and advanced algorithms, businesses can anticipate future trends, optimize decision-making, and drive better outcomes. From sales forecasting and customer behavior prediction to risk assessment and supply chain optimization, the applications of predictive analytics are vast and varied. However, successful implementation requires a commitment to data quality, the right tools and techniques, and a deep understanding of the business problems being addressed. As predictive analytics continues to evolve, businesses that invest in these capabilities will be better positioned to make informed decisions, mitigate risks, and capitalize on emerging opportunities.

CHAPTER 9

Overcoming Common Challenges with Analytics

Analytics has become a cornerstone of business strategy in today's data-driven world, enabling organizations to make more informed decisions, uncover hidden insights, and optimize operations. However, despite the many advantages that analytics offers, businesses often encounter several challenges when implementing and integrating analytics into their decision-making processes. These challenges can range from data quality issues and lack of expertise to difficulties in interpreting insights or gaining organizational buy-in. This chapter delves into the most common challenges businesses face when leveraging analytics and offers practical solutions for overcoming these obstacles. By addressing these challenges head-on, organizations can harness the full potential of analytics and create a more data-driven approach to decision-making.

Challenge 1: Data Overload and Data Quality Issues

One of the most significant challenges businesses face with analytics is managing the sheer volume of data generated daily. With advancements in technology, companies now have access to an unprecedented amount of data from various sources, including customer interactions, sales transactions, social media activity, and Internet of Things (IoT) devices. While this influx of data offers valuable insights, it can also lead to data overload, where businesses struggle to manage and make sense of the information. Compounding this issue is the problem of data quality. Inaccurate, incomplete, or inconsistent data can lead to flawed analysis and poor decision-making. In fact, data quality issues are one of the primary reasons why analytics projects fail to deliver meaningful insights.

Solutions to Data Overload and Quality Issues

To overcome data overload, businesses must adopt strategies for prioritizing and managing data. Data governance frameworks play a critical role in ensuring that data is properly categorized, organized, and accessible to those who need it. Organizations should focus on collecting data that is relevant to their business objectives, rather than attempting to capture every available data point. Implementing data management platforms or data lakes can also help businesses store and manage large datasets, allowing for more efficient analysis. Addressing data quality issues requires a multi-faceted approach. Businesses should implement robust data cleaning practices to remove duplicate, outdated, or inaccurate records. This involves regularly auditing datasets, standardizing data formats, and filling in missing information. Additionally, companies can use data validation tools to ensure that new data being collected adheres to predefined quality standards. By focusing on both reducing data overload and improving data quality, businesses can create a solid foundation for effective analytics.

Challenge 2: Lack of Analytical Skills and Expertise

Another major challenge businesses face is the skills gap related to data analytics. While analytics tools have become more accessible, the ability to derive meaningful insights from data often requires specialized knowledge in areas such as statistics, machine learning, and data science. Many organizations struggle to find or develop talent with the necessary expertise to build, interpret, and maintain advanced analytical models. This lack of expertise can lead to underutilization of analytics tools, misinterpretation of data, or even failure to implement analytics solutions effectively. As a result, organizations may miss out on valuable insights that could drive better decision-making and improve business performance.

Solutions to the Analytics Skills Gap

To bridge the skills gap, businesses should invest in upskilling and reskilling their workforce. Offering employees training opportunities in data analysis, data visualization, and statistical methods can empower them to become more proficient in using analytics tools. Additionally, businesses can partner with external training providers or online learning platforms that offer specialized courses in data science and analytics. In some cases, it may also be beneficial to hire data scientists, data engineers, or data analysts with advanced expertise to lead analytics initiatives. These professionals can build complex models, guide decision-makers in interpreting insights, and ensure that analytics efforts are aligned with business goals. Hiring skilled data professionals can also create opportunities for internal mentorship, allowing employees with less experience to learn from experts.

Another solution is to leverage automated analytics tools. Many modern analytics platforms now offer user-friendly interfaces and pre-built models that simplify the analytics process. By reducing the technical complexity of data analysis, these tools enable employees without a data science background to perform basic to intermediate analyses and derive insights.

Challenge 3: Siloed Data and Lack of Integration

Data silos occur when data is stored in separate systems or departments, making it difficult for teams across the organization to access and share information. This fragmentation often leads to incomplete analyses, as decision-makers are unable to obtain a holistic view of the business. For example, a marketing team might have access to customer engagement data, while the sales team manages transaction data, and neither group can fully leverage the other's insights. Siloed data not only hampers collaboration but also undermines the effectiveness of analytics by preventing cross-functional teams from making data-driven decisions that consider all relevant information.

Solutions to Data Silos

To break down data silos, organizations must adopt an integrated data strategy. This involves consolidating data from multiple sources into a centralized platform or data warehouse, where it can be accessed and analyzed by different departments. Data integration tools such as ETL (Extract, Transform, Load) solutions and API integrations can facilitate the process of connecting disparate data systems, ensuring that data flows seamlessly across the organization. Additionally, businesses should encourage cross-functional collaboration between teams that manage different data sources. By fostering a culture of data sharing, organizations can ensure that insights from one department can inform decisions in another. For example, the marketing and sales teams can work together to analyze customer behavior data and develop more targeted campaigns. Another solution is to implement data democratization initiatives, which make data accessible to employees across the organization, regardless of their role. Tools like self-service analytics platforms enable non-technical users to access and analyze data without relying on IT or data science teams, further reducing the impact of data silos.

Challenge 4: Resistance to Change

Despite the growing importance of analytics in modern business, many organizations still encounter resistance to change when implementing data-driven decision-making processes. This resistance often stems from a lack of understanding about the value of analytics or concerns that data-driven approaches might disrupt established workflows. Employees who are accustomed to making decisions based on intuition, experience, or tradition may be reluctant to adopt new tools or rely on data to guide their actions. Similarly, managers who feel threatened by the transparency and accountability that comes with data-driven decision-making may resist efforts to implement analytics initiatives.

Solutions to Overcoming Resistance

To overcome resistance to change, organizations must focus on building a data-driven culture that promotes the use of analytics at all levels. This starts with leadership buy-when senior executives and managers embrace analytics and demonstrate its value, employees are more likely to follow suit. Organizations should also provide training and education on the benefits of data-driven decision-making. By showing employees how analytics can improve efficiency, reduce risks, and drive better outcomes, businesses can alleviate concerns and increase adoption. Additionally, offering hands-on training with analytics tools can help employees become more comfortable using data in their daily work. Incentivizing data-driven behavior can also help reduce resistance. For example, businesses can reward teams or individuals who successfully leverage analytics to achieve key performance goals. By recognizing and celebrating data-driven successes, organizations can reinforce the importance of analytics and encourage further adoption.

Challenge 5: Difficulty Interpreting Data and Insights

While many businesses are adept at collecting and analyzing data, one of the most common challenges is interpreting insights in a meaningful way. Analytics often produces a wealth of information, but if decision-makers are unable to understand or act on these insights, the data becomes less valuable. For instance, an analytics report might reveal trends in customer behavior, but if the insights are presented in a confusing or overly technical manner, it may be difficult for teams to take appropriate action. Another challenge is the potential for data misinterpretation. Even with accurate data and robust models, incorrect conclusions can be drawn if the insights are misunderstood or taken out of context. This can lead to poor decision-making and ineffective strategies.

Solutions to Interpreting Data

One of the best ways to ensure that data insights are understood and acted upon is to invest in data visualization tools. Tools like Tableau, Power BI, and Google Data Studio allow businesses to present complex data in the form of intuitive charts, graphs, and dashboards. Visualization makes it easier for decision-makers to grasp trends, patterns, and anomalies at a glance, enabling them to make more informed decisions. Another important solution is collaboration between data teams and business units. Data scientists or analysts should work closely with decision-makers to provide context around the data and explain the implications of their findings. By aligning data insights with business objectives, organizations can ensure that the data is actionable and relevant to key decisions. Additionally, businesses should focus on building data literacy across the organization. Data literacy programs can help employees at all levels understand how to read, interpret, and act on data insights. This involves training employees not only in analytics tools but also in critical thinking skills that allow them to assess the validity and relevance of the data they're analyzing.

Challenge 6: Integration of Advanced Analytics Tools

As analytics becomes more sophisticated, businesses are increasingly adopting advanced tools such as machine learning, artificial intelligence (AI), and predictive analytics. However, integrating these advanced tools into existing business processes can be challenging. Many organizations struggle with the technical complexity of deploying AI models, or they lack the infrastructure needed to support large-scale data processing. Additionally, advanced analytics often requires significant computational resources and specialized expertise, both of which may be beyond the capabilities of smaller businesses or organizations with limited budgets.

Solutions to Integrating Advanced Analytics

To successfully integrate advanced analytics tools, businesses should first assess their infrastructure and ensure that they have the necessary computational power and data storage capabilities. Cloud-based platforms such as AWS, Microsoft Azure, and Google Cloud offer scalable solutions for businesses that need to process large datasets or run complex machine learning models without investing in expensive hardware. Next, organizations should focus on building or acquiring the necessary expertise. This may involve hiring data scientists, engineers, or AI specialists to develop and deploy models. Alternatively, businesses can partner with third-party vendors or analytics firms that specialize in advanced analytics tools. Finally, organizations should start small by implementing pilot projects to test the effectiveness of advanced analytics tools before scaling them across the organization. By starting with manageable projects, businesses can refine their processes, identify any technical challenges, and build confidence in the value of advanced analytics.

Analytics offers immense potential for improving decision-making, optimizing operations, and driving business growth. However, to fully realize these benefits, organizations must overcome several common challenges, including data overload, skills gaps, siloed data, and resistance to change. By adopting the right strategies—such as data governance frameworks, upskilling programs, and fostering a data-driven culture—businesses can successfully navigate these challenges and create a more effective, data-driven approach to decision-making. As businesses continue to rely on data as a strategic asset, overcoming these challenges will be critical to staying competitive in an increasingly data-centric world. By addressing issues such as data quality, interpretation, and integration, organizations can unlock the full potential of analytics and achieve long-term success.

CHAPTER 10

The Future of Analytics in Strategy

The landscape of analytics is rapidly evolving, with new technologies, methodologies, and tools shaping the way businesses approach decision-making. As data continues to grow in both volume and complexity, organizations that harness the power of advanced analytics will be better positioned to thrive in a highly competitive and dynamic market. However, staying ahead requires more than just using the current tools; it involves anticipating and embracing the future of analytics. This chapter explores the emerging trends and innovations that are driving the future of analytics. From artificial intelligence (AI) and machine learning to real-time data processing and advanced data visualization techniques, we will examine how these developments are shaping the future of analytics in business strategy. We will also discuss the challenges organizations may face as they adapt to these changes and the steps, they can take to remain competitive in a data-driven world.

The Role of Artificial Intelligence and Machine Learning

One of the most transformative trends in the future of analytics is the increasing integration of artificial intelligence (AI) and machine learning (ML). While these technologies are already widely used in predictive analytics and automation, their potential is far from fully realized. AI and machine learning offer the ability to analyze massive datasets at unprecedented speeds, identify complex patterns that would be impossible for humans to detect, and make autonomous decisions based on data-driven insights.

Autonomous Decision-Making

The future of analytics will likely see a shift from data-driven decision-making to autonomous decision-making. With advances in machine learning, businesses will be able to deploy AI systems that can not only analyze data but also make decisions in real time without human intervention. For instance, AI-powered systems could be used to automatically adjust pricing in response to changes in demand, manage supply chain operations, or personalize customer experiences based on behavioral data. Autonomous decision-making will enable businesses to respond more quickly and effectively to changes in the market, reducing the time it takes to make critical decisions. This level of automation can improve efficiency, reduce human error, and allow companies to focus on higher-level strategic initiatives. However, the rise of autonomous decision-making also presents new challenges. Organizations must ensure that their AI systems are transparent, ethical, and aligned with their overall business goals. Moreover, businesses will need to invest in the governance of AI systems to avoid unintended consequences, such as biased algorithms or incorrect decisions resulting from flawed data.

Enhanced Predictive and Prescriptive Analytics.

Machine learning is expected to continue enhancing both predictive and prescriptive analytics. Predictive analytics, which forecast future outcomes based on historical data, will become more accurate and sophisticated as AI models are trained on larger datasets and more complex variables. As these models evolve, businesses will be able to anticipate changes in the market with greater precision, enabling them to adjust their strategies proactively.

In addition, prescriptive analytics, which not only predicts future outcomes but also provides recommendations on how to achieve desired results—will become more widely adopted. For example, an AI-powered prescriptive model could analyze data on consumer behavior and suggest the optimal marketing strategy to maximize sales, while also providing insights on how to allocate resources most effectively. This ability to recommend actionable steps based on predictive insights will revolutionize how businesses plan and execute their strategies.

Real-Time Data Processing and Streaming Analytics

The growing importance of real-time data processing is another trend that will shape the future of analytics. As businesses become increasingly digital, the need for real-time insights has never been greater. Whether it's monitoring social media activity, tracking website performance, or managing financial transactions, organizations must be able to process and analyze data in real time to stay competitive. Streaming analytics is a key technology that enables real-time data processing. Unlike traditional batch processing, where data is analyzed in chunks after it has been collected, streaming analytics allows businesses to process data as it's generated. This means that organizations can receive immediate insights and respond to events as they happen.

For example, a retailer using streaming analytics might be able to detect a sudden spike in demand for a particular product and immediately adjust its supply chain to ensure that the product remains in stock. Similarly, financial institutions can use streaming analytics to monitor transactions for signs of fraud in real time, enabling them to prevent fraudulent activities before they cause significant damage. The future of analytics will see increased adoption of streaming analytics as businesses look to capitalize on the growing availability of real-time data. To achieve this, organizations will need to invest in infrastructure that can handle the demands of high-speed data processing and ensure that their analytics systems are capable of delivering actionable insights in real time.

Democratization of Data and Analytics

As analytics becomes more integral to business strategy, there is a growing need to democratize data—making it accessible to employees at all levels of the organization, not just data scientists or IT professionals. The future of analytics will involve empowering more employees to leverage data in their day-to-day decision-making, enabling organizations to become more agile and data driven. The democratization of data will require businesses to invest in self-service analytics tools that allow non-technical users to access, analyze, and interpret data without needing to rely on specialized teams. Tools such as Power BI, Tableau, and Qlik Sense are leading the way in making analytics more user-friendly, offering intuitive interfaces that enable employees to create their own reports and dashboards. In addition to making data more accessible, businesses will need to invest in data literacy programs to ensure that employees have the skills to interpret and act on the data they are using. As more employees are empowered to make data-driven decisions, organizations can improve their ability to respond to changes in the market, innovate more rapidly, and optimize their operations across departments.

Advanced Data Visualization and Storytelling

Data visualization will continue to evolve as businesses look for more effective ways to communicate insights and tell compelling stories with data. Interactive dashboards, augmented reality (AR) visualizations, and natural language processing (NLP) are just a few of the technologies that are transforming how data is presented and understood. Interactive dashboards allow users to explore data in real time, adjusting filters and parameters to view different aspects of a dataset. This interactivity enables decision-makers to delve deeper into the data and uncover insights that might not be immediately apparent from static reports. Businesses will increasingly adopt these dashboards to improve their ability to communicate insights to stakeholders. Additionally, augmented reality is poised to become a key tool in data visualization. By overlaying data visualizations on real-world environments, AR can provide more immersive and engaging ways to interpret complex information. For example, a financial analyst could use AR to visualize stock performance trends in a 3D space, providing a more intuitive understanding of the data. Natural language processing is another technology that will play a critical role in the future of data visualization. By enabling users to interact with data using natural language queries (e.g., "What were last month's sales in New York?"), NLP makes analytics more accessible to non-technical users. This capability will further democratize analytics, allowing more employees to gain insights from data without needing advanced technical skills.

The Integration of Analytics with Emerging Technologies

The future of analytics will be deeply intertwined with other emerging technologies, such as blockchain, the Internet of Things (IoT), and quantum computing. These technologies are expected to significantly impact how data is collected, processed, and analyzed.

Blockchain and Data Integrity

One of the key challenges in analytics is ensuring the integrity and security of data. Blockchain technology offers a solution to this challenge by providing a decentralized, immutable ledger that ensures data is tamper-proof and verifiable. This is particularly valuable for industries that handle sensitive data, such as finance, healthcare, and supply chain management. By integrating blockchain with analytics systems, businesses can improve data transparency and trust. For example, in supply chain analytics, blockchain can be used to verify the authenticity of data at each stage of the process, ensuring that the information used in decision-making is accurate and reliable.

IoT and Predictive Analytics

The Internet of Things (IoT) is generating vast amounts of real-time data from connected devices, sensors, and machines. This data presents new opportunities for businesses to enhance their predictive analytics capabilities. By analyzing data from IoT devices, businesses can gain deeper insights into operational efficiency, equipment performance, and customer behavior. For example, manufacturers can use predictive analytics to monitor machinery in real time, identifying potential maintenance issues before they lead to costly downtime. Retailers can analyze data from IoT-enabled smart shelves to optimize inventory management and improve customer experiences. As IoT continues to expand, the future of analytics will be defined by the ability to harness and analyze data from billions of connected devices, leading to more intelligent and proactive decision-making.

Quantum Computing and Big Data Analytics

Quantum computing is expected to revolutionize the field of big data analytics by providing the computational power needed to solve complex problems that are currently beyond the capabilities of classical computers. Quantum computers have the potential to process massive datasets exponentially faster than traditional systems, enabling businesses to analyze vast amounts of data in real time. For example, in industries such as finance, healthcare, and logistics, quantum computing could be used to optimize investment portfolios, accelerate drug discovery, and improve supply chain logistics by analyzing multiple variables simultaneously. While quantum computing is still in its early stages of development, it holds the promise of transforming how businesses approach analytics, particularly for solving complex problems that require massive computational resources.

The future of analytics is bright, with emerging technologies such as AI, machine learning, blockchain, and quantum computing set to redefine how businesses collect, process, and analyze data. As organizations continue to embrace data-driven decision-making, the ability to stay ahead of these trends will be critical to maintaining a competitive edge. However, navigating the future of analytics requires more than just adopting new technologies. Businesses must also focus on democratizing data access, fostering a data-driven culture. By embracing these principles, organizations can unlock the full potential of analytics and drive strategic success in an increasingly complex and data-driven world.

GLOSSARY

Algorithm: A set of instructions or rules designed to solve a specific problem or perform a computation. In the context of analytics, algorithms are used to analyze data and generate predictions or insights.

Analytics: The process of collecting, processing, and analyzing data to uncover patterns, trends, and insights that inform business decisions.

Artificial Intelligence (AI): A branch of computer science that focuses on creating machines or systems capable of performing tasks that typically require human intelligence, such as problem-solving, decision-making, and language understanding.

Big Data: Large and complex datasets that traditional data processing tools are unable to handle effectively. Big data is characterized by its volume, velocity, variety, and veracity, and requires specialized tools for analysis.

Blockchain: A decentralized, immutable ledger that records transactions across many computers in a way that ensures data integrity and security. Blockchain is often used in industries that require high levels of transparency and data authenticity.

Business Intelligence (BI): The technology-driven process of analyzing data and presenting actionable information to help executives, managers, and other business professionals make informed decisions.

Cloud Computing: The delivery of computing services—such as storage, processing power, and networking—over the internet. Cloud computing enables organizations to access resources on demand without needing to maintain physical infrastructure.

Customer Relationship Management (CRM): A system for managing a company's interactions with current and potential customers. CRM tools help businesses organize, automate, and synchronize sales, marketing, and customer service activities.

Data-Driven Decision-Making: A decision-making process that relies on data analysis and interpretation to guide business strategies, rather than intuition or personal experience.

Data Governance: The set of policies, procedures, and standards that govern how data is managed, accessed, and protected within an organization to ensure its accuracy, security, and usability.

Data Lake: A storage system that holds vast amounts of raw, unstructured data in its native format. Data lakes are often used to store data for future analysis and processing.

Data Literacy: The ability to read, understand, analyze, and communicate data effectively. Data literacy is a critical skill for employees in data-driven organizations.

Data Quality: A measure of how accurate, complete, consistent, and timely data is. High-quality data is essential for producing reliable insights and making informed decisions.

Data Silos: A situation where data is isolated in different departments or systems, preventing cross-functional teams from accessing or sharing valuable insights.

Data Visualization: The graphical representation of data in the form of charts, graphs, maps, or dashboards to make complex information more understandable and actionable.

Descriptive Analytics: A type of analytics that focuses on summarizing historical data to understand what has happened in the past. It typically involves reporting and dashboards.

ETL (Extract, Transform, Load): A data integration process that involves extracting data from various sources, transforming it into a suitable format, and loading it into a data warehouse or another target system.

Forecasting: The process of predicting future trends or outcomes based on historical data and analytical models. Forecasting is used in various business functions, such as sales, finance, and operations.

Internet of Things (IoT): A network of physical devices, vehicles, appliances, and other objects embedded with sensors and software, allowing them to collect and exchange data over the internet.

Machine Learning (ML): A subset of artificial intelligence that allows systems to learn from data and improve their performance over time without being explicitly programmed. Machine learning is widely used in predictive analytics.

Natural Language Processing (NLP): A field of AI that enables machines to understand, interpret, and respond to human language in a way that is both meaningful and useful. NLP is commonly used in chatbots, virtual assistants, and data query systems.

Predictive Analytics: A branch of analytics that uses historical data, machine learning, and statistical models to forecast future outcomes, trends, or behaviors.

Prescriptive Analytics: A type of analytics that goes beyond predicting future outcomes and provides recommendations on how to achieve desired results. It suggests the best course of action based on the analysis.

Regression Analysis: A statistical technique used to model the relationship between a dependent variable (the outcome) and one or more independent variables (the factors that influence the outcome).

Real-Time Data Processing: The ability to collect, process, and analyze data as it is generated, allowing businesses to respond to events and changes in real time.

Self-Service Analytics: Analytics tools and platforms that allow non-technical users to access, analyze, and interpret data without needing assistance from IT or data science teams.

Streaming Analytics: The process of analyzing and processing data in real time as it is generated, rather than in batches after it has been collected. Streaming analytics is critical for businesses that need to respond quickly to changing conditions.

Time Series Analysis: A statistical technique used to analyze data points collected over time to identify patterns and forecast future trends.

Value-at-Risk (VaR): A financial metric used to estimate the potential loss that a company could incur due to market fluctuations over a specific time period. VaR is commonly used in risk management.

www.ingramcontent.com/pod-product-compliance
Lightning Source LLC
LaVergne TN
LVHW091357210726
843527LV00001B/26

* 9 7 8 7 7 5 9 4 8 1 4 6 5 *